O K

COP   20

J929.909
     Parrish, Thomas D.
       The American flag. Illus. with
     photos., prints and drawings. Simon,
     c1973.
       101 p. Illus. (part col.).
       Traces the history of the American
     flag from the arrival of the first
     explorers to the present day. Grades 6-
     9.
                              RCN 768839-3

     1. Flags. I. Title.

The
American
Flag

The American Flag

by
Thomas
Parrish

Illustrated with photographs, prints and drawings

A CORD COMMUNICATIONS BOOK
SIMON AND SCHUSTER   NEW YORK

Contents

The
American
Flag

1

Symbol in the Sky

THE WORLD was watching and listening. More than six hundred million people in forty-nine countries—Americans, Europeans, Asians, Africans, Australians—had gathered in front of television sets, and many millions more were following the great story on their radios.

It was July 20, 1969. In the United States it was afternoon, Sunday afternoon. But it was not a quiet Sunday. There had never been one like it in the history of the world, and there would never be one like it again.

Two men held the world's attention: Neil Armstrong, a boyish-looking test pilot, and Edwin (Buzz) Aldrin, a scholarly United States Air Force colonel. They sat in a spacecraft called *Eagle,* and they were descending toward the surface of the moon. If everything went according to the careful and complex plans, they would soon be the first human beings ever to set foot on a part of the universe other than the earth.

But first, a safe landing had to be made. The moment for it was approaching. It was the first high point of a voyage of dis-

The giant space vehicle carrying Astronauts Armstrong, Aldrin and Collins lifts off from the launch pad on the morning of July 16, 1969. The vehicle is as tall as a thirty-six-story building.

covery that had begun four days before, when Armstrong and Aldrin and the third member of their crew, Astronaut Michael Collins, had been hurled into space from Launch Pad 39A at Cape Kennedy, Florida. Finally, they had come very close to the moon, only about seventy miles above its surface, and their vehicle, Apollo 11, had gone into orbit around it. After completing eleven circuits, the space ship had divided into two crafts. One called *Columbia,* was piloted by Collins. It had remained in orbit, to observe, direct and wait for the other craft. That one, *Eagle,* was the lunar module, the crablike vehicle that would land on the moon's surface. Now it was carrying Neil Armstrong and Buzz Aldrin away from Apollo 11's high orbit. When it passed above the moon at a height of only fifty thousand feet, its crew fired the

This is the official emblem of the Apollo 11 mission. It was worn by the three astronauts. The eagle is one of the most famous symbols of the United States.

propulsion system—small rocket engines that could alter its course and speed—and *Eagle* began its direct descent.

It was almost onto the moon, only about fifty feet above it. But the landing spot Armstrong and Aldrin were heading for, guided by *Eagle's* automatic equipment, proved to be a huge crater, with slanting sides strewn with rocks. The possibility of a crash landing grew greater with every second. Armstrong, who was the captain, quickly switched off the automatic landing system and took over manual control. For a minute and a half he maneuvered *Eagle* away from the crater toward a clear area. Dust, stirred up by *Eagle's* engine, swirled on the moon's surface.

Then a light flashed on—the contact light. This meant that the sixty-eight-inch probes, or feelers, hanging from *Eagle's* stilt-like legs had touched ground. One second later, the astronauts cut off the descent engine. Then the world got the word from the moon: Armstrong radioed to Mission Control Center in Texas, "The *Eagle* has landed."

They had made it! Human beings were now on the moon. But the millions and millions of people in front of their television sets were waiting for an even more dramatic moment. Everyone wanted to see Neil Armstrong descend the ladder from *Eagle* and actually place his foot on this alien body in space.

After a careful check of their landing craft, and preparation for eventual takeoff, Neil Armstrong emerged from the hatch of *Eagle* and began lowering himself down the ladder. At this point, he turned on an outside television camera which began transmitting the first actual pictures from the moon. By means of this camera, television viewers around the world were able to see Armstrong's bulky boot make its first contact with the moon's surface. As he stepped down, the astronaut said, "That's one small step for a man, one giant leap for mankind."

Then, after Armstrong had tested the ground for nineteen minutes, he was joined by Buzz Aldrin. The two men first set up another television camera, one that could provide a picture of a wide scene. Next, with all the world watching, they performed an

Astronaut Buzz Aldrin stands beside the American flag planted by the moon explorers.

official task: they produced an American flag and planted it in the ground. In doing this, they were carrying out an age-old ritual of explorers. In earlier eras, when such adventurers landed on a new island or a new continent, they would unfurl the flag of their king and claim the newly discovered territory in his name. New France, New Spain or New Britain, they would call it.

But things were somewhat different on the moon. In the first place, the airless environment provided no breeze to stir the folds of a flag. The Stars and Stripes planted on the moon therefore had to be made rigid; it was stiffened with wire so that it would stand out. In the second place, of course, the witnesses made up the largest audience that had ever seen such an event take place.

A third difference was particularly important. The astronauts did not claim possession of the moon for the United States. The United States had never claimed any such right. In fact, the United

States, the Soviet Union and other countries had signed a treaty making the moon *terra nullius*—no man's land. It was to be open to exploration by anyone who could get there. In fact, the astronauts left a plaque saying, WE CAME IN PEACE FOR ALL MANKIND.

It is perfectly plain, then, that the American flag was not planted as a sign that the United States was claiming the moon for itself. But if that was not the purpose, what was? Was the flag intended to be a kind of calling card? Was it put there as evidence of devoted effort and spectacular achievement? Was it boasting, a way of saying, "Look at what we have done"? It was probably something of each one of these things. Many persons in the government and across the country as well were extremely proud of the historic journey of the astronauts. But others objected to the planting of the United States flag on the moon. Some persons simply did not like the entire project and did not believe that the government should spend money for such purposes.

Different points were raised by others. They approved of the flight, and they approved of placing a flag on the moon. But they did not want it to be the American flag. They asked why it should not be the flag of the United Nations. They argued that use of this flag would suggest to the whole world that the moon belonged to everybody and not to any one nation.

To some, this might have seemed to be a pointless controversy—a lot of fuss about a three-foot-by-five-foot piece of cloth. If the argument had been simply about cloth, that would have been true. But the discussion went far deeper than that. It was an argument about a *symbol*.

In its most basic meaning, a symbol is simply an object of any kind that stands for something else. A cross represents a religion. A crown represents a king. A picture of the Rock of Gibraltar represents an insurance company. A tiger represents Princeton University. All these are symbols. They are not religions, or kings, or insurance companies, or universities. They *stand for* these things. When you see the symbol, you think of the thing it stands for.

Some persons objected to the placing of the United States flag on the moon. Instead, they preferred this blue-and-white flag, the symbol of the United Nations.

The official and most widely known symbol of a nation is its flag. Every nation has a flag. Often, in fact, a nation has several different flags. They serve different purposes, but each one is still the symbol of the nation. A country may have other symbols, too. England, for instance, is often represented in newspaper cartoons by John Bull, a stout, sturdy fellow who is supposed to suggest qualities believed to be typically English. All Americans are familiar with Uncle Sam, the bearded Yankee. And another American symbol, the eagle, provided the name for the astronauts' moon craft.

But in the world today, flags are the most important symbols that nations have. People love them and hate them, fight for them and tear them to shreds. Flags are treated as though they were more than symbols—as though they actually possessed the qualities they are supposed to stand for. But such object worship is not new. It has existed since man first began using one thing to represent another.

2

Flags
and Feelings

WITHOUT knowing it, you may at some time or other have been a *vexillary,* and you may have a friend who is a *vexillophilist.* Before you disagree, stop and think whether you've ever had occasion to carry a flag (that would make you a vexillary) or whether you know somebody who likes to collect flags (if you do, your friend is a vexillophilist) . Both these words are based on the Latin word *vexillum.* This fact would naturally lead you to believe that *vexillum* is the Latin word for "flag." But that is not exactly the case, for a simple reason: the ancient Romans did not have flags as we know them. The closest they came to our present-day flags was the banner they called a *vexillum.* It was carried by a soldier mounted on a horse and was a square piece of cloth hung from a crosspiece fastened to a spear. It could not float or fly in the wind as a true flag does.

In addition to these square banners the Romans also had identifying symbols called *standards.* These were small solid figures mounted on poles. Sometimes they depicted gods, of whom the Romans had a great many. Others were little statues of horses,

16

wolves and other animals that were important in Roman legends. When the Roman Empire was at its height, each legion of the army carried an eagle as its standard. But the Romans had no banner that could have been called the national flag.

Actual flags as we know them seem to have been first used in China and India. Indian soldiers, mounted on elephants, lumbered into battle carrying flags of various colors. And as long ago as 1000 B.C. the Chinese had flags with figures of tigers and dragons and other symbolic creatures on them. The ancient Chinese regarded flags as so important, in fact, that it became a crime just to touch the bearer of a king's flag. And if a king's flag fell to an enemy, it meant that the king himself had lost the battle. The symbol not only stood for the king, but was thought to be as important as the monarch himself.

In an interesting way, flags seem to have arrived in the European world at about the time when there was a particular need for them. Most likely, the idea of a freely waving banner mounted on a pole or a staff was brought to Europe during the Middle Ages by Crusaders returning from the Holy Land.

Partly as a result of the Crusades, which took Europeans many hundreds of miles from their homelands, the continent of Europe was stirring into new life in the late Middle Ages. People were looking outward and becoming adventurous and were beginning to explore the world. One of the most famous explorers was Christopher Columbus. But there were many others. As men sailed farther and farther from home, and ocean trade routes became more and more important, a growing need was felt for an easy way to identify the ships.

Already, on land, European kings and queens flew flags called royal standards—large and elaborate flags that floated over their castles and were carried with them when they traveled. These flags were personal symbols. Where the flag was, in most cases, there the king was. Such personal standards obviously would not do for ships. Most were too big, too complicated in design and too hard to identify at a distance. And they were supposed to serve a dif-

The symbols of European kings and queens were called royal standards. The standards shown here were flown by rulers of England. Usually each king or queen made personal changes in the standard on ascending the throne.

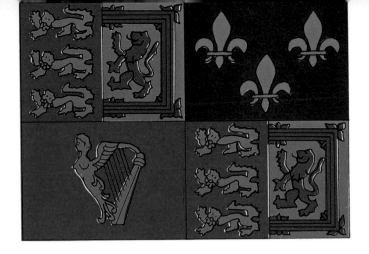

ferent purpose. What was needed at sea was a simple, bright-colored flag that could be seen from far off.

In addition to their elaborate royal standards, the English had—since the Crusades—used such a flag. It consisted of a red cross, called the cross of St. George, on a white background. These colors, red and white, came to be recognized at sea as the colors of England. Other countries began using equally simple symbols.

It was at this time that countries were starting to become nations, each with its own community of interests. Up until now, a country had been regarded essentially as the property of its king or its most powerful nobles. The change from loose organization

Hundreds of years ago, English ships carried this famous red-and-white flag—the cross of St. George.

to a more unified governmental structure did not happen all at once, of course; in some countries it barely happened at all. But when and where it did occur, the meaning of the flag changed along with it. The flags of kings began to be the flags of countries. As the 1500s turned into the 1600s, old symbols took on new meanings.

Then came the 1700s. And in this, the eighteenth century, two great events shook the world. Because of these events, flags became more important than they had been before. They became symbols with new kinds of meanings. In the first of these great events, the people living in a group of colonies in the New World rebelled against their mother country, England, and asserted that they possessed certain rights and were entitled to certain freedoms not because of their nationality or their social class or their wealth but simply because they were people. They would fight, they said, until they secured these rights. The colonists declared themselves to be independent, and one of the signs of this independence was a new national flag—the deliberately chosen symbol of the people of a nation. This was the Stars and Stripes.

The Stars and Stripes was the first national flag in history to be chosen by representatives of the people of a country, rather than by its ruler.

The second great event was the French Revolution. It took place only a few years after the American Revolution. Here the people rebelled against their royal family. They too drew up a declaration—the famous Rights of Man. And they adopted a new flag—the famous Tricolor. It had three wide vertical stripes, one red, one white, one blue. It was supposed to stand for liberty, equality and fraternity, or brotherhood. These were the ideals proclaimed by the revolutionaries, and the Tricolor has remained the flag of France.

Because both the American Stars and Stripes and the French Tricolor were the flags of people who had overthrown oppressive rulers and created new governments, they were copied by other revolutionary countries. Both flags were red, white and blue. Both incorporated stripes in their designs. In the minds of people around the world, the colors and the stripes became symbols of independence and liberty. They seemed quite different from the crowns and the black double eagles of the royal flags. A striped red-white-and-blue flag seemed to promise freedom and a better life.

All of the changes that have taken place in the world since the American Revolution have, in fact, made the Stars and Stripes a kind of grandfather among national flags. This is true even though the United States is often called a young country. In Europe national flags have come and gone. Countries have changed governments or merged into other countries or simply disappeared. Historic empires have vanished from the map. In Asia and Africa and Latin America new countries and new governments have created new flags. In the modern world, as soon as a new government comes into being it calls for a new official symbol. This has happened many times around the world in the past twenty years.

So the American flag has become an old and familiar symbol. But people do not always agree about what this symbol stands for. It is the official identification of the United States, of course. But what traits and qualities does it represent? In recent years there has been a great deal of discussion of this question—some of it calm, some of it very hot.

Only a few years after the United States flag was created, the people of France adopted this famous flag—the red-white-and-blue Tricolor.

New countries mean new flags. From these flagpoles outside the United Nations in New York fly the symbols of three young nations: Zambia (left), Malta and Malawi (right).

As a physical object, the American flag is the same flag for everybody. But because it is a symbol, it is more than an object. The feelings that people have about it depend, in the first place, on tradition—on the ideas and attitudes that the flag has always been supposed to represent. But the way that people feel about the flag at any particular time also depends on the way they feel about the United States itself at that time. It depends on what they think about politics and international affairs and history. When the country is united in a cause, the flag is an admired and honored symbol. When there is great debate and dissent, there is disagreement about the flag.

In a newspaper advertisement saluting Flag Day, an automobile dealers' association expressed this point of view: "When you display the Flag, you're saying a lot about yourself. You're saying that you have faith in the future of our country. It also means that you want to stand up and be counted. As members of the community, we're concerned that some Americans appear to have forgotten the true meaning of the Flag. The Flag itself may remind them."

But this advertisement does not actually say what the writers believe the "true meaning" of the flag to be. Probably they had in mind the ideas contained in the Pledge of Allegiance to the flag: "I pledge allegiance to the flag of the United States of America and to the Republic for which it stands, one nation under God, indivisible, with liberty and justice for all."

Some persons have expressed a different point of view. They feel that the Pledge of Allegiance is a better statement of aims and purposes than of actual fact. They propose that the pledge be taken to the flag as the symbol of a nation "*seeking* liberty and justice for all."

Still others simply do not appear to take the flag very seriously. They make tents and skirts out of it, and wear it on T-shirts and the seats of their jeans.

But there are two groups of people who have treated the flag as a most important symbol indeed—two strongly opposing groups.

Often today, the United States flag is not treated as a serious symbol of the nation. Instead, it is used in the design of clothing. It turns up on jackets, headbands, parkas, and even sneakers.

OUR FLAG

"LOVE IT OR LEAVE"

Many patriotic organizations distribute bumper stickers like this one.

One is made up of persons who have expressed their opposition to United States policies by ripping up American flags and burning them in public streets. The others are persons who have decorated their cars with decals bearing sentiments about the flag and slogans like AMERICA—LOVE IT OR LEAVE.

These public arguments and fights—and the casual wearing of the flag as a piece of clothing, too—would be amazing to students of sixty and seventy years ago. In their classes they learned by heart poems like this:

> O flag of our ~~Union~~ *Country*,
>   To you we'll be true,
> To your red and white stripes,
>   And your stars on the blue;
> The emblem of freedom,
>   The symbol of right,
> We children salute you,
>   O flag fair and bright!

The sight of an American flag being burned in the streets by a crowd of demonstrators would have horrified President Benjamin Harrison. Back in the 1890s he expressed this strong belief: "God pity the American citizen who does not love the flag; who does not see in it the story of our great, free institutions, and the hope of the home as well as the Nation."

As you can see, this red-white-and-blue symbol of the United States and its people arouses strong emotions. And it has stirred up strong feelings of one kind and another throughout its two centuries of existence. It has stood not only for the character and personality of the United States but for American history, too. It has been an important part of that history. Or, to put it another way, it has an important history of its own.

3

A New
World

IT HAD BEEN a rough day at sea, the roughest of the whole
five-week voyage. The weather for the journey had mostly been
good, the sailing smooth. But trouble had come from the crews of
the three ships that were sailing westward together. As the days
had passed, the sailors had grown discontented. Many of them had
wanted to return home. Some of them, of course, were simply
frightened. They thought they were approaching the edge of the
world, where dragons and other monsters might lie in wait for
them. Educated persons knew better, to be sure; they knew the
world was round. But ships' crews were not made up of educated
men.

Earlier in the day, encouraging evidence had been sighted.
Little sandpipers had flown close to the admiral's ship, the *Santa
Maria,* and a green branch had floated nearby. The birds and the
branch *must* mean that land was almost within reach. But it was
true that birds had been seen several days before, and yet there had
been no land.

The admiral stared into the night. There, suddenly—a spot of

An old lithograph shows Christopher Columbus saying goodbye to King Ferdinand and Queen Isabella just before leaving on his voyage of discovery. He sailed from Palos, Spain, on August 3, 1492.

light across the distance! He was sure of it. It looked, he later wrote in the journal of the voyage, like a "small wax candle." He called the crew of the *Santa Maria* together. They must all keep a sharp lookout, he told them.

At two o'clock on the morning of October 12, 1492, the lookout on the *Pinta,* the lead ship, gave a shout: *"Tierra!* Land!" The captain of the *Pinta* ordered a cannon fired. This was the signal that had been agreed upon.

The boom of the cannon was an exciting and welcome sound to the admiral. Now land could be dimly detected at a distance of seven or eight miles. But it could not be approached until dawn.

When day broke, the admiral could see a green island lying behind a barrier of reefs. It was, he thought, a Japanese island; he
did not know that there was a continent of any kind in the ocean
between Europe and Japan.

The ships anchored offshore, and with the captains of the
Pinta and the *Niña,* Admiral Christopher Columbus was rowed
to the island in the *Santa Maria*'s landing boat. The journal says:
"The Admiral brought out the royal standard, and the captains
went with two banners of the green cross, which the Admiral flew
on all the ships as a flag." The first of these flags, the royal standard, was the flag of King Ferdinand and Queen Isabella (or
Ysabel) of Spain, the sponsors of the expedition. It consisted of
two castles (for the old kingdom of Castile) and two lions (for
the old kingdom of Leon). The other flag was a personal flag
specially created for Columbus.

As the admiral, the greatest explorer of his own day, came
ashore, he was watched by silent natives of the island. Timidly
they stood back as the members of the Spanish party kissed the
earth, put up a crucifix, knelt before it and gave thanks to God.
What could all this mean? The natives did not know that the island they called Guanahani had now become San Salvador. And
they could have no idea what the castles and lions stood for and
what was happening when the leader of the party took possession
of their home in the name of Ferdinand and Isabella of Spain. The
first flag of a European country now flew in what was to become
known as the New World. It would soon have plenty of company.

Actually, one particular European flag had probably appeared
in America several hundred years earlier. But there is no definite
proof of this, and in any case the flag was not the flag of a country. It was the banner flown by the Vikings on their excursions into
the Atlantic from their Scandinavian home. It consisted of a
raven on a white field. Since the raven itself is a black bird, this
was probably a black-and-white flag. But even if the Vikings did
bring such a flag to North America, it had no influence on any
other flags or on anything that happened later. The Vikings were

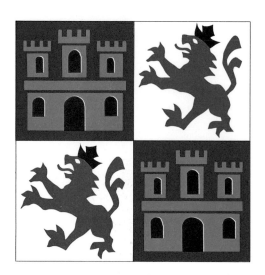

One of the flags carried ashore by Columbus was this royal standard of his patrons, King Ferdinand and Queen Isabella. Columbus claimed possession of the New World in the name of the king and queen.

When the Spanish party landed, they gave thanks to God for their safe journey through the perils of the ocean.

The first flag to fly anywhere in North America may have been the raven banner of the Vikings, who carried it on their raiding expeditions into the Atlantic.

adventurers and raiders. Whatever they did in America was not written down. News of it was not spread across Europe. It did not lead to conquest and colonization or to trade and further discovery.

While it may be true to say that the Vikings were the first flag-bearers in North America, it was Columbus whose discovery made the greatest impact. The historic importance of his voyage was that it led to further exploration and to permanent European settlement. It changed the world. It directed the eyes of Europe to the west.

Portugal, France and England soon joined the Spanish in exploring the New World. Later, flags of the Netherlands, Sweden and Russia were carried inland by exploring parties and were raised at forts and trading posts. These flags are of interest to us because they flew over parts of what are now the fifty states, but most of them did not make direct contributions to the development of the flag of the United States. Where our flag of today is concerned, they are more like distant relatives than like parents or grandparents.

But some of these flags are very much in the family—ancestors, in one way and another, of the Stars and Stripes. The most important of these were the flags brought to America by the British and those that were created here by the people in the British colonies. By the time of the American Revolution, British flags flew from Massachusetts to Georgia. Great Britain was the mother country against which the thirteen colonies rebelled. It is only natural that the flags that floated over these colonies and flew from their ships had the greatest influence on the flag of the independent United States.

For more than a century after Columbus, the most common British flag in the New World was the flag of St. George—the red cross on a white field. "St. George's banner broad and gay," it was called. This was really not a *British* flag but was an *English* flag, because there was not yet any kingdom of Great Britain. England and Scotland were separate countries, and St. George's flag had come to be regarded by everybody as the national flag of England. St. George was the saint usually identified with England.

In the early 1600s the British flag picture became more complicated. This happened because, in 1603, King James I—the king after whom the King James Version of the Bible is named—came to the throne of England. He was already king of Scotland, where he was known as James VI, and Scotland—like England—had its own flag and patron saint. The Scottish saint was Andrew, the brother of St. Peter. His cross was white and the field (the background) of the flag was blue. St. Andrew's cross was made of diagonal lines, so that it looked like an X that has been somewhat flattened out. Flag specialists—vexillologists—call this kind of cross a *saltire*. St. Andrew's cross was not a saltire by accident. According to legend, Andrew was crucified on a cross of this shape. He is supposed to have said that he was not worthy of being put to death on an upright cross like the one on which Jesus was crucified.

The difference in shape between the right-angled cross of St. George and the saltire of St. Andrew turned out to be extremely convenient for the royal heralds, King James's flag designers. Early in his reign the king decided to adopt a flag showing that he was ruler of both England and Scotland. This decision brought about the creation of the Union Flag. The idea of the Union Flag was to symbolize the union of the two crowns—two kingdoms with one king. If you will look at St. George's flag and St. Andrew's flag and then at the flag that resulted when the two were put together, you will see that the heralds did an ingenious job of carrying out their assignment. This new flag was adopted in 1606. Now there was one flag with three colors—red, white and blue.

In his proclamation announcing the new flag, King James talked about some of the reasons behind it and laid down rules for displaying flags on ships. The king observed that "some difference hath arisen between our subjects of South and North Britain, traveling by seas, about the bearing of their flags." Because of this, King James said, he had decided that "from henceforth all our subjects of this isle and kingdom of Greater Britain" should "bear in their main-top the Red Cross, commonly called St. George's Cross, and the White Cross, commonly called St. Andrew's Cross, joined together, according to a form made by our heralds." Further, the king said, "in their fore-top our subjects of South Britain shall wear the Red Cross only, as they were wont, and our subjects of North Britain in the fore-top the White Cross only, as they were accustomed." To emphasize these rules, the king added this warning: "They will answer the contrary at their peril."

As King James's proclamation explains, the Union Flag was first created for ships, as the king's symbol. It did not replace the separate flags of St. George and St. Andrew, which were to be flown as always by ships of "South Britain" and "North Britain." The mainmast, to which King James assigned the Union Flag, was the position of greatest honor, where a ship should wear its most important flag—"wear" means "display" when flags on ships are being discussed. But the masters and crews of ships had ideas of

When King James VI of Scotland became king of England in 1603, he brought along the Scottish flag—the white cross of St. Andrew on a blue background.

their own. As time went on, the custom grew up in the navy of wearing a small version of the Union Flag on the bowsprit of a ship—the spar that projects from the bow. This flag came to be called the *jack,* probably because "jack" is an old English word meaning "small." No one is sure of this, however.

But whatever the name of the jack originally meant, ships began to fly two types of identifying flags—the *ensign* and the *jack.* Nowadays, these two flags can easily be distinguished on a ship. The jack is flown from a small staff at the bow; the ensign—a larger flag—from a staff at the stern. The purpose of both is to show the nationality of the ship. The ensign is actually the basic flag for this purpose; the jack, being smaller, is a sort of helper. In fact, the *canton* of the ensign—the upper left-hand part—is often exactly the same as the entire jack. In the United States Navy, for instance, the ensign is the Stars and Stripes; the canton of the ensign is the blue rectangle with fifty stars. The jack consists simply of the blue rectangle with the stars.

In the days of King James and the kings who succeeded him, things were not quite so precise. And sailing ships, with their various masts, offered many different possibilities for the wearing of flags. The most interesting development was that the Union Flag itself became the jack. This is of course the name by which we know this famous flag and its somewhat changed successor—the Union Jack.

This flag is most familiar to us as the flag flown by the British government on land. It is different now from the Union Jack of King James's time because in 1801 it acquired a third cross—a red saltire—to stand for Ireland. As you can see, the task of fitting this third cross into the Union Jack must have been a real challenge to the flag designers.

The British Union Flag, usually called the Union Jack, is made up of the red cross of St. George (for England) plus the white cross of St. Andrew (for Scotland). It also has a third cross (for Ireland), which you can see as a red X broken in the center.

Through much of the seventeenth century, the kings tried to reserve the Union Flag for their own ships—that is, for the navy rather than for privately owned merchantmen. King Charles I issued a proclamation to this effect in 1634. But a more important move in this direction came about thirty years later, when King Charles II authorized an ensign for both the navy and the merchant fleet. This flag was the Red Ensign. It is a very important flag in American history as well as British history. It was the grandfather of the Stars and Stripes.

4

From Red Ensign to Grand Union

THE COLONISTS used the British Red Ensign as the basis for a number of flags that were flown only in America. Discussion of the history of flags is sometimes confusing because the same flag will have different names at different times or different flags will have the same name. The second point is true in the case of the Red Ensign. During the colonial era, two important flags bore this name. One grew out of the other, but they were nevertheless different.

The first Red Ensign was actually an English ensign. There was nothing Scottish about it. It consisted of St. George's cross on a white background as the canton; the field was solid red. During the 1600s there were various flags with the cross of St. Andrew in the canton, but they do not seem to have had any influence on flags in the colonies. The main reason is simply that, though England and Scotland were technically separate countries, England was far richer and more powerful than its sister kingdom and the colonies were English colonies. The English navy and the English merchant fleet were the ones that counted.

The first Red Ensign flew during the 1600s. Its canton was the English flag (St. George's cross); the field of the flag was solid red.

In 1707 a new Red Ensign was born. Here again, the creation of a new flag symbolized a new development in history. This time the new development was the actual joining together of England and Scotland into a united kingdom. No longer was there any need for separate ensigns. Now—for official purposes, at least—there were only British flags, not English flags and Scottish flags. The canton of all ensigns became the Union Jack—a flag within a flag. The Red Ensign now consisted of a red field with the Union Jack in the corner. More and more, the Red Ensign came to be regarded as the merchant ensign (today this is its official purpose). But on warships as well as merchant ships, it was seen in colonial harbors from Boston down the coast to Charleston.

The first Red Ensign, the one with St. George's cross in the canton, was flown by merchant ships sailing from the colonies as well as by those sailing from ports in the mother country. All were regarded as English vessels. On land, however, some interesting things happened to the Red Ensign. One of the most curious developments occurred in Massachusetts. There, in the 1630s, some devout Puritans became concerned about the presence in the Red Ensign of St. George's cross. The question touched them directly because the Red Ensign was carried as the colors of their local regiment of troops. What worried the Puritans was the fear that the cross might be a sort of symbol of idolatry—the kind of religious relic that their beliefs sternly forbade. Led by a man named John Endicott, they removed St. George's cross from the colors. The result was a very plain flag. It had a solid white canton and a solid red field.

This Endicott flag was the first of a long line of flags created by tinkering with the Red Ensign. These were flags in which the field remained untouched while different kinds of changes were made in the canton. One of the most widespread and longest-lived was the flag usually called the New England flag. It was the Red Ensign, including St. George's cross—with one small detail added

The Red Ensign turned up in a variety of forms. One of the most popular versions was this flag, called the New England flag. It was the Red Ensign plus a tiny pine tree in the corner of the canton.

In another version of the Red Ensign, the pine tree grew so big that it took up the whole canton, and St. George's cross was dropped out.

in the upper left-hand corner of the canton: a small green tree, usually a pine tree.

The New England flag is particularly interesting because it is an early example of a distinctive American contribution to the English flags. It was a positive development, instead of the negative change that was made simply by the removal of St. George's cross. It is interesting, too, because pine trees went on to play quite a part in American flags. They, and other plants and animals, were a new kind of element in flags. Previously, flags had been based on European history and legend and on the elaborate principles of the science of heraldry. This New England flag appears to have been flown at sea as an ensign as well as displayed on land. There seems to have been a similar flag that simply used a pine tree in place of St. George's cross in the canton. It is very hard to be sure just what these flags of two and three centuries ago looked like and just where they were flown. But the latter pine-tree flag is believed by some specialists to have been the one flown by the colonial troops at the Battle of Bunker Hill in 1775.

In the family tree of the Stars and Stripes, one set of non-British flags is specially worthy of mention: flags brought to America by Dutch explorers and traders. These were striped flags, unlike the British flags, and they were in two sets of colors. One was orange, white and blue; the other was red, white and blue. Flags of the latter type thus combined two features of our present American flag, the colors and the stripes. There is actually no evidence to show that the American rebels sat down one day in 1775 or so and decided to borrow these features from a Dutch flag that some of them might possibly have seen. There is not even any evidence that they thought about the Dutch flag at all. Perhaps the Dutch banner was only distantly kin to the American flag, or was a nonrelative that merely happened to have some features in common with it. Whatever the case, there was a Dutch flag in New York not long after the English had arrived at Jamestown and well before the *Mayflower* brought the Pilgrims to Plymouth. The *Mayflower*, incidentally, could conceivably have worn the Union Flag but most likely flew St. George's cross—whether or not all the passengers approved of it.

The Dutch brought striped flags to the New World. Some were orange, white and blue. Others were our familiar red, white and blue.

This flag is sometimes known as the colonial jack, sometimes as the escutcheoned jack. "Escutcheon" is the word for the shield that appears in the center.

In 1701, the English government created a flag that is called the colonial jack or, sometimes, the escutcheoned jack. It was supposed to be flown by merchant ships that were sailing under orders from colonial governments and were for this reason regarded as public ships rather than private ships. The colonial jack was simply the Union Jack with a shield—an escutcheon—added in the center, where the crosses intersect. The shield was blank. What is noteworthy about this flag is really the fact that it was a sort of official flag for all the American colonies. It was intended to distinguish colonial ships, whatever the colony they were sailing for, from ships sailing from the home country.

More and more, as the eighteenth century advanced, the colonies drew apart from Great Britain. They developed interests that were different from those of the mother country. Disputes and hostilities flared and flamed. What was good for one, economically, was often bad for the other. What one regarded as rights, the other seemed to regard as unjust demands. This was not a simple, continuous series of events, it must be remembered. Sometimes relations between the colonies and Great Britain improved. In a war against France, they fought together. And, certainly, not everybody in the colonies shared the feelings of hostility toward the mother country. There were strong differences of opinion about public affairs then, as there are today.

What resulted from all the disagreements and quarrels was, of course, the American Revolution. The Revolution, and the events leading up to it, brought into being a fresh variety of flags—flags of regiments, of cavalry troops; flags of colonies and localities; ensigns and jacks, for use at sea; flags that perhaps flew only in a single battle or from a single ship. The pine tree was joined as a colonial symbol by the fiercely American rattlesnake. Liberty trees—trees under which patriots gathered to hold meetings—also appeared as elements in flags. Poles called liberty poles served as

In the 1770s, patriots put up flagstaffs called liberty poles. People who were opposed to British rule of the colonies gathered around them.

LIBERTY AND UNION

The colonists used the Red Ensign for their own purposes in many ways. One way, as in the famous Taunton flag, was to put patriotic slogans on it.

staffs from which flags of defiance flew. Some of these flags were versions of the second Red Ensign—versions with words blazoned on them. LIBERTY AND UNION cried the famous flag at Taunton, Massachusetts.

In this fall of 1774, when the Taunton flag was unfurled, a group of fifty-five delegates from the colonies met in Philadelphia. This was the first Continental Congress. The name was an imposing one for the representatives of a strip of seacoast on the edge of a great continent that was mostly untracked wilderness. Perhaps this was a public-relations touch, designed to impress the government in London. In any case, the first Continental Congress petitioned the British government for a "redress of grievances"; that is, the gentlemen in Philadelphia were seeking a peaceful way to work things out between Great Britain and the colonies. The answers from London were not favorable.

By the next fall—1775—a great deal had happened. Battles had been fought at Lexington and Concord and at Bunker Hill. George Washington, a wealthy Virginia planter, had been chosen commander in chief of the volunteer army that was fighting the British troops in Boston. Washington's courage and determination had made a great impression on the second Continental Congress, which named him to the office. Certainly a strong sense of duty was a prominent part of Washington's character; the assignment was not a promising one.

In the fall of 1775 the members of the second Continental Congress were trying to deal with a thousand problems at once, and all of them were new problems. Everything they did was being done for the first time. Some students of flags have lamented the fact that this Congress was not preoccupied with the designs of flags, rules for displaying them and other such questions. Working under the pressures of a thirteen-hour daily schedule, the delegates

This old engraving shows an artist's view of the Battle of Bunker Hill, fought at Boston between British regulars and New England soldiers.

The Continental Congress needed a strong and courageous commander in chief for the inexperienced colonial army. It found its man: George Washington, a Virginia planter.

simply had to take first things first. When a question concerning a flag became critical, then it would be answered.

At this time Congress had not yet decided that the United Colonies must become a new country, separate from the mother country. But they agreed that they must go on using whatever force they could muster until the British government granted the Colonies the rights they claimed. They must wage war.

This would not be a war like the European wars of that day, with masses of highly trained soldiers engaged in sophisticated military maneuvers and fighting prescribed battles as if they were chess games. The Colonies simply did not have that kind of army. Nor did they have the armaments that would have been needed to conduct that kind of fighting. So the war on land would be irregular. The war would be irregular on the sea, too. It was on the sea, in fact, that the United Colonies had their best chance of damaging the enemy—not by fighting naval battles but by raiding British supply and merchant ships. In this kind of warfare, Britain would have a great deal to lose, the Colonies almost nothing.

Silas Deane, a gentleman from Connecticut, was a member of the Continental Congress. He later represented the United States in France.

The need for armaments was urgent. Washington's troops outside Boston were short of muskets and cannons, shot and gunpowder. Even if the commander in chief succeeded in keeping his volunteer soldiers at a fighting pitch, they could do little if they were short of weapons. They could hang on, perhaps, but they could not win victories.

Then, in October, exciting news reached Philadelphia. Friends of the American rebels reported from London that two ships were leaving England with orders to sail across the Atlantic to Quebec, in Canada. The news was exciting because these were munitions ships—ships carrying weapons and gunpowder for the British army in North America. They were cargo ships, not warships. They were not armed for fighting.

Some members of Congress—John Adams among them—began thinking about a bold plan. They proposed that Continental ships be sent out to capture the merchant ships before they reached America. Since the United Colonies had no navy at all, no warships and no sailors trained in sea warfare, the plan was daring. It was daring, too, because carrying it out would be another historic "first" for the Continental Congress. The act of seizing a British ship on the open sea would be a truly ringing insult to King George III and his ministers. It would be even more of one, probably, than the battles that had been fought at Lexington and Concord and Bunker Hill. In those battles, for one thing, the Americans could claim that they were simply defending themselves and their homes.

Some of the delegates felt that the plan was somewhat *too* daring. A "mad" and "wild" and "visionary" project, they called it. But on October 13, Congress voted to set up a naval committee. John Adams was one of the members, and for his efforts in this cause has since been called the "father of the United States Navy."

These actions of the Continental Congress, however, could not result in any navy that would be ready in time to sail in search of the two British supply ships, even though they would be at sea for several weeks. To solve the problem, Congress turned to Gen-

The British king during the American Revolution was George III. He and his ministers took various steps that angered the colonial patriots.

eral Washington. The commander in chief was a man of drive and energy. He was ahead of Congress; he had been ahead of it for more than a month. Realizing that the siege of Boston was getting nowhere and that supplies must be found, he had already acted on his own. He had begun to create a navy.

This important step was possible because the army regiment from Marblehead, Massachusetts, was made up of experienced sailors. They were, Washington said, "soldiers who have been bred to the sea." He made them sailors officially, and he gave army commissions to the commanders of two ships. On September 2, 1775, he issued orders to his first captain, Nicholson Broughton of

Marblehead. They were bold and sweeping and clear: the commander in chief was perfectly willing to slap British faces. Captain Broughton was to search for any ships "in the service of the Ministerial Army" (the idea of the Americans being that the ministers, not the king, were the true enemies of the Colonies). He was "to take and seize all such vessels laden with soldiers, arms, ammunition or provisions." He was to avoid battles, because supplies—not victories—were the object.

These moves by General Washington seem to have made Congress more aware of the importance of war at sea—and, perhaps, more willing to risk British anger. They not only approved the commander in chief's actions, they asked him to fit out several more ships. The general was already doing so. He succeeded in rounding up several fishing schooners and merchant ships—the *Lynch,* the *Lee,* the *Warren* and others. During the second week of October, Washington received the news about the two British munitions ships. This was exactly the kind of mission he had had in mind when he had begun setting up his little fleet—"Washington's Cruisers" and "Washington's Navy," it is called. The general notified his ship commanders. The vessels were, he wrote to Captain Broughton, "two North Country brigantines of no force"—that is, unarmed two-masted ships. Broughton and his fellow captains proceeded to search for the two merchantmen, which—if we can judge by all the letter-writing and planning that went on while they were at sea—must have been slow vessels indeed.

Washington's Cruisers were really the first ships of the United States Navy, because they were the first ships commissioned by the authority of the Continental Congress. But there was no flag of the United Colonies that could serve as the ensign for this navy created by the army. Yet the ships must have a standard flag, for two good reasons. In the first place, as General Washington's secretary said, it would be a "signal by which our vessels may know one another." It would also be a sign by which the ships of other countries could recognize them. It would show that they belonged to a regular force and were not pirates, outlaws of the sea. There was really a third reason, too: a flag would help the

AN APPEAL TO HEAVEN

"Washington's Cruisers," the little fleet collected by the commander in chief, flew a flag with the familiar New England pine tree.

men develop a feeling of working together in a great cause.

Because these were New England ships with New England crews, the pine tree of New England seemed an appropriate symbol for them to wear, and the pine-tree flag was hoisted as their ensign—the first ensign flown by American warships. It was a simple flag, though there seem to have been various versions of it. It had a white field with a green pine tree in the center. Above or below the tree was the line APPEAL TO HEAVEN. Sometimes this line is given as *"an* appeal to heaven." The idea, like the pine tree, was characteristic of New England. It expressed the Colonials' faith that God saw the justice of their cause.

The *Lee,* one of the cruisers flying the pine-tree flag, sailed on November 4. This ship had the best record of Washington's Cruisers, and late in November the commander in chief received word that the *Lee* had snared one of the big prizes. It had sighted and closed on one of the lumbering British supply ships, the *Nancy.* The unarmed *Nancy* had been no match for it. And the *Lee's* crew had not been disappointed. In the hold of the *Nancy* were two thousand small firearms, tons of musket shot, a load of flints (for firing muskets) and a gigantic thirteen-inch brass mortar that weighed more than a ton. Washington's soldiers later nicknamed this weapon "Congress." Whether this bit of humor was prompted by the mortar's brass, its wide-open mouth, the noise it could produce or some other feature, we do not know.

While Washington's Cruisers were hunting in the sea-lanes, their pine-tree flags flying in the November winds, the naval, or marine, committee of Congress was working to put together the beginnings of an official Continental navy. By the end of November, several ships with at least partial crews had been assembled in the Delaware River at Philadelphia.

During this same month the marine committee had chosen a commander in chief for this infant United States Navy: Esek Hopkins of Rhode Island. Hopkins was a salty, sharp-tongued veteran of forty years as a captain of merchant ships. He was given the title of commodore, and in the coming months he acquired a flag to go with his rank. Although the flag played no part in the development of the Stars and Stripes, it was one of the famous flags of our history. It was yellow, with a coiled rattlesnake and the motto

The Gadsden flag, flown as a jack by the Continental navy, used the American rattlesnake as a symbol of defiance of the British.

DONT TREAD ON ME

At the end of 1775, the Continental navy began to take shape. One of its first officers—and its first hero—was the legendary John Paul Jones. At this time he was twenty-eight years old.

DONT TREAD ON ME. It is usually called the Gadsden flag, after a member of Congress who was particularly fond of it, Colonel Christopher Gadsden.

On December 3, 1775, Commodore Hopkins arrived in Philadelphia to take command of the new Continental fleet. His flagship was to be the *Alfred,* a 350-ton vessel that was in the process of being made ready for war. (A flagship is the ship that carries the commander of a squadron or a fleet.) Here, the commodore was introduced to a short, stocky and firm-jawed young man of twenty-eight who would soon be famous in both America and Britain—John Paul Jones, the United States Navy's first great hero.

But Mr. Jones was not yet a hero. At this time he was awaiting Congressional confirmation of his commission as a lieutenant in the brand-new navy, and it soon came—the first such commission.

On this day—December 3, 1775—occurred what was probably the most important flag event of the United Colonies up till that time. A new flag had come into being; the Continental Colors, it was called, although it had not been adopted formally by Congress. It represented not a single colony or a single region but all thirteen of the United Colonies. By his own testimony, John Paul Jones had the privilege of raising it. It was the first ensign to fly over the first ship of the regular United States Navy.

This painting by the noted artist N. C. Wyeth shows John Paul Jones hoisting the first American navy ensign, the Continental Colors, in December 1775.

The ensign that John Paul Jones is believed to have raised is known by a number of names, including Grand Union Flag and Cambridge Flag. It was the familiar Red Ensign with white stripes added to it.

This flag was not yet the Stars and Stripes, because the Colonies still considered themselves part of Great Britain (and the navy was not yet the United *States* Navy). But because it was the emblem of *all* the colonies, it was more important than the pine-tree flag or the rattlesnake flag or any of the others that had gone before it.

"I chose to do it with my own hands," wrote John Paul Jones. The flag that was raised by those hands has become known to us by other names besides the Continental Colors. It is called the Grand Union Flag and the Great Union Flag. It is also called the Cambridge flag, because on New Year's Day 1776 General Washington ordered it raised on a pole near his headquarters outside Boston. Yet the navy used it as the ensign a month before it was raised by the army—though it is quite possible that Washington was consulted in the design of it.

Except for one feature—but it was a most important feature —this flag was the same as Britain's Red Ensign. It was not a distant relative of the Red Ensign but a son or daughter, a direct and immediate descendant. What the Colonials did was convert the Red Ensign into an emblem of the thirteen United Colonies. They did this by placing six white stripes across the red field, producing a total of thirteen stripes, red and white. The flag that resulted was a symbol of the United Colonies, but the Union Jack in the canton showed that the Colonies still thought of themselves as British, as subjects of the king. A British intelligence agent in Philadelphia described the flag to his superiors as "English colors but more striped." For more than a year and a half, these colors would serve first as the flag of the United Colonies and then as the flag of the United States.

Ever since people began to study the history of the American flag, they have wondered and debated about the source of the stripes in the Grand Union Flag. What, they have asked, led the Colonials to use stripes as the distinguishing feature of the flag? Nobody can be sure of the answer, but several facts probably were involved.

In the first place, there were various striped flags in existence at the time. Some were local flags within the colonies. Another was the flag of the East India Company, which not only had stripes but had the Union Jack as the canton. Too, there had been the striped Dutch flags mentioned earlier. Nobody knows which of these influenced the designers of the Grand Union Flag, but certainly the idea of stripes in a flag was not completely new to them.

The second point is a practical one. Shipowners and other persons who needed to fly flags already had the Red Ensign on hand, and flag bunting, or cloth, was scarce. It came, in fact, from England. In emergencies, any kind of cloth could be made into flags, of course. But it was good sense to design a new ensign that could be made directly from an old one.

Another reason goes along with these two and may be the best single answer. It is simply that the use of thirteen stripes, representing the thirteen colonies, was a logical move as a step away from the Red Ensign. If it had practical virtues too, so much the better!

5

"A New Constellation"

ONE DAY in 1870, about a hundred years after the American Revolution, a gentleman named William J. Canby told an extremely interesting family story to the members of the Pennsylvania Historical Society. It concerned his grandmother, a Philadelphia lady named Elizabeth Griscom Ross.

Sometime in June of 1776, it seemed, she had received a group of unusually important visitors in her upholstery shop, a business she had continued to operate after the death of her husband. One of the callers was her husband's uncle, Colonel George Ross. Another was Robert Morris, a rich contributor to the Colonial cause. The third was very distinguished indeed: General George Washington, commander in chief of the Continental Army.

What these gentlemen wanted, Mr. Canby said, was a flag. His grandmother, who was then a young lady of twenty-four, had made shirt ruffles for General Washington and he therefore knew that she was an accomplished seamstress. Mrs. Ross is supposed to have said that she had never made a flag but would try. The visitors

If Betsy Ross actually made the first United States flag, this is how she might have looked while working on it. But the Betsy Ross story, most historians agree, is legend, not fact.

then produced a sketch. Mrs. Ross looked it over and made some criticisms and suggestions, and Washington then drew it again in accordance with her ideas. What Washington drew was the design of a flag having thirteen stripes and a canton with thirteen stars—the first Stars and Stripes.

This is the Betsy Ross story, America's most famous flag legend. In Philadelphia today, at 239 Arch Street, you can see Mrs. Ross's house very much as it appeared in 1776. It is now called the Flag House. And in 1952, to commemorate the two-hundredth anniversary of Betsy Ross's birth, the U.S. Government issued a three-cent stamp showing the legendary lady stitching a flag while Washington and his distinguished companions look on.

This all seems to make the story quite official. But the problem is that there is no evidence to back up Mr. Canby's charming account, and there are all kinds of reasons to question it. Very few historians believe it at all. There *was* a Besty Ross, and later in

the Revolution she did make flags. These are facts on which everyone agrees. But Mr. Canby and other members of his family are
the *only* sources for the story that she made the first Stars and
Stripes. There is no record of it, in any form, written at the time
of the Revolution itself—no official orders, no notes, no bills. And,
scholars point out, the United Colonies were not even looking for
a new flag in June 1776. The Continental Congress had not yet
decided to vote for independence. The truth seems to be that all
peoples and nations have myths and legends about their early
days, and the Betsy Ross story is one of ours.

Actually, in this June of 1776 the Grand Union Flag, or
Continental Colors, still had a year to wave. Even though independence was declared during the next month, on July 4, Congress
took no action concerning a flag. The gentlemen were as busy as
ever—possibly busier. Not until June 14, 1777, would a new flag
be adopted.

*The U.S. Government made the Betsy Ross story official: Some years
ago, the Post Office Department honored Mrs. Ross's two-hundredth
birthday anniversary with this stamp.*

On July 4, 1776, the Continental Congress declared that the United Colonies were free from their allegiance to Great Britain. This engraving shows the signing of the Declaration of Independence.

In the meantime, the Continental Colors would be busy, too. It had been in constant use ever since it had been created. On January 1, 1776, General Washington had used this "union" flag for a highly symbolic purpose. It was a tense time; with men who had enlisted in the army for one year now going home and uncertain volunteers arriving, the future was dim and doubtful. Most of the general's soldiers still were New Englanders. Men had not come forward from the other colonies as he had hoped they would. So, in a brave gesture, a kind of public-relations effort in behalf of the army, Washington declared that it now was "in every point of view entirely continental" and "in compliment to the United Colonies" ordered the Grand Union Flag raised to greet the new year and the new army.

On June 14, 1777, Congress adopted this resolution: *Re-solved, that the Flag of the united states be 13 stripes alternated red and white, and the Union [the canton] be 13 stars white in a blue field representing a new constellation.* This is all that the official journal of Congress had to say about the new flag. Congress did not even make provision about the arrangement of the stars. The record does not say who introduced the resolution, what the origin of the design was or anything else at all concerning the flag. It is just as though Congress had waved a magic wand and the Stars and Stripes appeared.

The stripes were already present in the Grand Union Flag, of course. But many historians have tried to discover who suggested replacing the Union Jack in the corner with the starry canton. Stars were a new element in flags, although a few starred flags may have been in existence at the time. Scholars disagree about this. But the use of stars in other kinds of symbols was well known—in the coats of arms of nobles, for instance, and in official seals. Nobody knows who proposed stars for the United States flag. Scholars have discovered a bill for the design submitted by Francis Hopkinson, a signer of the Declaration of Independence who was chairman of the Navy Board and is known to have been an artist as well. But Congress did not honor his bill—and that is just about all we know. There is one curious fact about the stars in the American flag: according to the principles of European heraldry, they are not stars at all, because they have five points instead of six or more; a five-pointed "star" stood for a rowel, the wheel part of a knight's spur. But there is no evidence that the leaders of the American Revolution were worried about this refinement.

Now, in the summer of 1777, the navy had a new ensign. For almost a year after the Declaration of Independence, it had continued to sail under a flag that included the Union Jack of Britain. Why Congress decided to act at this particular time, we don't know. Most likely, the same kinds of reasons operated in 1777 as operate today. Enough requests and criticism from enough people led to action. Certainly it was not very logical for American ships and forts to fly the flag of the country from which Americans had declared independence, even if that flag was only the canton of the American flag.

In its resolution, Congress referred to the new element in the flag as the *union*. The canton of the Red Ensign had been a union too. It had represented the union of England and Scotland. This union no longer had anything to do with the United States. So a new symbol of union took its place—the thirteen stars "representing a new constellation." This new union completed the transformation of the Red Ensign. If the Grand Union Flag was the child of the Red Ensign, the Stars and Stripes is its grandchild.

The changes took place step by step, as we have seen, until the red in the stripes was the only element of the Red Ensign that remained in the American flag. The long process of development that had begun hundreds of years before, with the cross of

Who designed the first Stars and Stripes (shown here)? Nobody knows. The Revolutionary patriot Francis Hopkinson submitted a bill, claiming to have done the work while chairman of the Navy Board, but Congress did not pay him. Actually, we do not even know how the stars were arranged.

The Stars and Stripes may have been first carried in battle in the Revolution at the Battle of Bennington, from which this flag takes its name. The "76" is a famous feature of this early American flag.

St. George, was complete. After 1777 the number of stars in the American flag would change. For a time, the number of stripes would change, too. But the Stars and Stripes had been born. The British Union Jack itself had one more important change to undergo—the addition, in 1801, of the red saltire that represents Ireland. Since then, these two flag cousins have become probably the world's most recognized flags.

In its early days, though, the Stars and Stripes was not always as recognizable as it is today. Congress had adopted a design by law, but not everybody followed it. On land, as was mentioned earlier, the flag did not often appear. When a national standard was run up over a building or carried in a battle, it was usually one that was hastily put together on the spot. There are various stories of coats and skirts being torn apart and reassembled as American flags, with variations in colors and design. In particular, since Congress had said nothing about the arrangement of the stars, they appeared as constellations of different shapes. Many pictures today show the stars arranged in a circle, but these are probably not very accurate.

Nobody knows when the Stars and Stripes was first used in a battle of the Revolution, but the distinction may well belong to the Bennington flag. This flag had seven white stripes and six red (instead of the customary opposite arrangement) and a very interesting canton: the stars were arranged in a semicircle, except for two in the top corners, and under the semicircle was the date "76"—the year of independence. This flag appeared at the Battle of Bennington, in Vermont, on August 16, 1777.

As the naval ensign, the Stars and Stripes did not always follow the Congressional prescription either. Even Benjamin Franklin seems to have thought that the stripes were supposed to be red, white and *blue.* So did John Adams, the father of the navy. And, as nearly as we can tell today, it was an ensign with red, white and blue stripes that was flown by the winning ship in one of the most ferocious sea fights of all time—a battle in which the victorious warship sank and the skipper had to transfer his flag to the ship that had been beaten. This skipper was John Paul Jones.

It happened in September 1779. In the two years since the first Flag Day, Jones had had adventures of all kinds. He had carried out a raid on a mansion near his boyhood home in Scotland (where his name had been simply John Paul—he added "Jones" to it after coming to America). He had captured a British warship, the *Drake.* He had received the first foreign salute to the Stars and Stripes. This occurred at Quiberon, France, and it was quite important to Jones. He was proud of the flag and had long wanted other countries to recognize it officially. After a little persuasion, a French admiral agreed to fire nine guns. John Paul Jones had wanted at least eleven, but finally decided that a nine-gun salute *was* a salute, even if it wasn't as big a one as he had wanted. This decision brought about a historic first for the Stars and Stripes.

In the late summer of 1779, Jones was no longer on the *Ranger,* the first warship under his command. He now com-

One of the true fathers of this country was Benjamin Franklin. During the Revolution he represented the infant United States in France, which became an ally of our nation. But Franklin seems to have once believed that the flag had blue stripes as well as red and white ones. The picture below shows the design as he thought of it.

Historians believe that the Benjamin Franklin–style Stars and Stripes probably flew from John Paul Jones's Bonhomme Richard *during its fierce battle with the British ship* Serapis. *It was in this battle that Jones said, "I have not yet begun to fight!"*

manded the *Bonhomme Richard,* which had been bought for him by the government of France, now an ally of the United States. He named the ship after Benjamin Franklin's famous character Poor Richard, whose wise sayings were very popular in Paris. *Bonhomme Richard* was simply the French version of the name.

"I intend to go in harm's way," Jones said when he received the ship, and that is exactly what he did. On the afternoon of September 23, 1779, the *Bonhomme Richard* and several accompanying ships were sailing off the North Sea coast of England. The closest point of land was a cape called Flamborough Head. In the middle of the afternoon the Americans sighted a group of merchant ships coming from the east. Like a convoy in World War II, they were guarded by a warship. This protector was His Majesty's Ship *Serapis* (se-RAY-pis) .

By seven o'clock or so, the two ships had come close together. Jones could see that the *Serapis,* a fifty-gun ship, was more heavily armed than his own. And it seemed to be faster, too. Yet he prepared for action. In order to deceive the *Serapis* and get as close as possible, he was flying a British ensign. When hailed by the Britisher, he hauled down the British flag and raised an American ensign with red, white and blue stripes. Then he immediately ordered a broadside—the firing of all the guns on one side. The *Serapis* returned a broadside of its own, and one of history's most renowned sea battles was on.

Disaster struck the *Bonhomme Richard* almost immediately. Two of its big guns exploded, and Jones decided that he could not risk using the others; they might do more damage to his own ship than the guns of the *Serapis* would. He tried to move in for hand-to-hand fighting but failed to grapple his ship to the *Serapis.* Then came a cry from the British captain: "Has your ship struck?"

Jones answered this demand for surrender with the resounding line "I have not yet begun to fight!"

This was a brave response, because the other ships in Jones's squadron were being no help at all. In fact, just the opposite was true. One of his captains, a Frenchman, was so jealous of his commander that as the battle went on he even attacked the *Bonhomme Richard.* But Jones continued to fight. Finally the two ships became locked together, yet the *Serapis*—at this point-blank range—continued to pour cannon fire into the *Bonhomme Richard.*

A member of Jones's crew crawled out on a yardarm extending over the decks of the *Serapis* and dropped a basket of hand grenades. These set off a store of the *Serapis*'s gunpowder. Then an amazing thing happened. Even though the *Bonhomme Richard* was actually in danger of sinking from battle damage and some of its crew wanted to strike the flag, they saw the ensign of the *Serapis* being lowered! The bloody battle—three hundred men were killed on the *Bonhomme Richard*—was over.

After a day and night of struggle to save it, the ship disappeared beneath the water on the morning of September 25. The red-white-and-blue-striped ensign was transferred to the *Serapis,* which John Paul Jones sailed to a port in the Netherlands. Under his vigorous leadership, the Stars and Stripes in any design had become an ensign of determination—a symbol that the small new United States intended to win its freedom.

6

The Star-Spangled Banner

I<small>T</small> was a foggy, drizzly night in mid-September 1814. A little sloop named the *Minden* lay quietly in the waters of Chesapeake Bay, near Baltimore. In front of the *Minden* a line of sixteen British ships fired cannons and rockets into the mist. On the deck of the little ship a man paced back and forth, watching the mighty bombardment. This man was a thirty-five-year-old Washington lawyer and amateur poet named Francis Scott Key.

He was not a participant in the fighting. Nor was he on board the *Minden* because he liked to watch bombardments. He was acting as a diplomat, a person who negotiates with representatives of foreign countries. He was doing this to help a friend and neighbor, an elderly doctor named William Beanes. Dr. Beanes was a prisoner of war. His captors were the British, who for two years had been engaged in a new war with the United States. They had landed five thousand troops at Washington and burned the Capitol and the White House. They had next planned to take Baltimore. The British fleet was supposed to help the land forces by attacking and knocking out Fort McHenry, which defended Baltimore against attack by sea.

This old engraving shows the British taking and burning the city of Washington in 1814.

The British general had apparently been in an optimistic mood that morning. He is supposed to have said, "I will have supper in Baltimore or in Hell." Neither he nor any other British soldier had supper in Baltimore that night. The general himself had been killed in the land attack, which was thrown back by the militiamen defending the town. The army of the British had failed. Everything now depended on their fleet.

Francis Scott Key had not expected to spend that night in the midst of a bombardment. With another American negotiator, he had come out to the British fleet during the preceding day. Their aim was to ask the British admiral to release Dr. Beanes. After some strong argument, the admiral had agreed: Dr. Beanes was an old man, and perhaps he had been wrongly taken prisoner.

But during the day the two Americans had heard the British officers discussing their plans to attack Fort McHenry. The admiral had therefore told them that they could return to the *Minden* but must stay behind the British lines until the battle was over.

Fort McHenry was only a small fortification, not a great citadel. Its chances of surviving a battering from sixteen heavy ships of the British navy did not seem very strong. But as the hours went by, it continued to return the British fire. Then the barrage stopped. Why? Had the British given up the attack? Or had the bombarded fort surrendered? Through the dark and the mist it was impossible to tell.

This is the actual flag that flew over Fort McHenry as Francis Scott Key waited for "the dawn's early light." It had fifteen "bright stars," fifteen "broad stripes."

Then came day—"the dawn's early light." And there, still waving, was the "star-spangled banner." Key was overjoyed. This was one occasion he *must* honor in a poem! As he was rowed ashore, he was writing swiftly on the back of an envelope. Later that same day he finished a final draft. And within the next few days his poem was printed and distributed. It was recited in the theater and even sung. It was called "The Defence of Fort McHenry." Everybody in Baltimore seemed to know it.

Key had written a poem, not a musical composition. But his words were quickly fitted to a tune that had long been familiar in America and Britain. It was, in fact, a tune that had been used earlier for another poem of Key's. This melody was usually known by the strange-sounding name "To Anacreon in Heaven," because an English poem with that title had been sung to it. Today very few persons remember either that name or the title that Key originally gave to his poem. The words and the music long ago blended into "The Star-Spangled Banner." Strangely, although "The Star-Spangled Banner" came to be regarded as the national anthem of the United States during the nineteenth century, it was not officially adopted until 1931. It seems that Congress never acts rapidly in matters concerning the flag.

The star-spangled banner that Francis Scott Key honored in his poem was different from the flag adopted by Congress in 1777. The flag flying over Fort McHenry had fifteen "broad stripes" and fifteen "bright stars." This had come about because of the admission of Vermont and Kentucky into the Union. If the original thirteen states each had a stripe and a star, the argument went, so should each of the two new states. The act providing for this change was passed in 1794 and went into effect May 1, 1795.

This fifteen-stripe flag flew through the presidencies of John Adams, Thomas Jefferson and James Madison (as well as through Washington's last years). It was the national flag when, under Jefferson, the United States acquired the vast Louisiana Territory from France. It was the ensign on the ships carrying the Marines "to the shores of Tripoli" in 1805, where they fought the pirates

The fifteen-stripe U.S. flag was Captain Stephen Decatur's ensign at Tripoli, North Africa, where Americans fought pirates who raided shipping in the Mediterranean Sea. In this vivid action, an American ship is in flames.

who raided ships in the Mediterranean Sea, and the Marines raised it in triumph over the pirate fortress of Derna.

If no more states had joined the Union, the fifteen-stripe flag would have been perfectly satisfactory. But after waving for only a year, it was outdated when Tennessee became a state. By the time Francis Scott Key wrote "The Star-Spangled Banner," two more states had come in: Ohio and Louisiana. Then, in 1816, came Indiana and in 1817 Mississippi. That made twenty states. And, as anybody who looked at the map could see, there might be many more of them. What should be done? If a new stripe were to be added for each new state, the stripes would become skinnier and skinnier. The original plan would be lost.

In 1818, Congress created this flag by reducing the number of stripes to thirteen—permanently—and providing for the addition of one star for each state admitted to the Union.

During these years, Congress took no action on the question. Many shipowners were no doubt happy to avoid the expense of changing flags as the number of states in the Union increased, although others added stars and stripes voluntarily. Finally, in 1817, a committee of Congress presented a solution to the star-and-stripe problem. It was the plan that has been followed ever since. The number of stars, said the committee, should always be equal to the number of states, symbolizing the Union as it is at any given time. The number of stripes should return to thirteen, symbolizing the number of states that had founded the Union. The act providing for this went into effect in 1818. It said that a new star should be added to the flag on the Fourth of July following the admission of a new state, since Independence Day is the nation's birthday.

By 1853 the number of stars had increased to thirty-one. This thirty-one-star flag was the ensign flown by the ships that carried out one of the most unusual missions in our navy's history—Commodore Matthew Calbraith Perry's voyage to Japan.

For several centuries the Japanese had lived in isolation from other countries. Their rulers wanted to have as little to do with foreigners as possible. But they could not control everything. From time to time, whether they liked it or not, shipwrecked sailors from fishing fleets would be washed up on the coasts of Japanese islands. Since they were foreigners, they were treated by the Japanese as enemies rather than as helpless victims of storms. The United States decided to protest this treatment.

There were other reasons, too, for American interest in

Commodore Matthew C. Perry's flag, the first U.S. ensign seen in Japan, had thirty-one stars in six lines, all but one line having five stars. As you can see, the line closest to the hoist had an extra star squeezed into it.

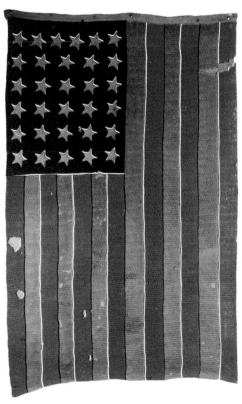

Japan. The development of steamships and the settling of the U.S. Pacific coast had focused new attention on the Far East. The United States was beginning to regard itself as a strong country, with thirty-one states and other territories besides. We were growing every day. Why should we not begin trading with our neighbors across the Pacific?

President Millard Fillmore saw no reason not to do so. He therefore decided to send a representative directly to the Emperor of Japan. The man he chose was Matthew C. Perry. Perry was the younger brother of the American naval hero of the War of 1812, Oliver Hazard Perry. In 1813, Oliver Perry had won the battle that gave the United States control of Lake Erie. The battle had also given the navy two famous sayings. Perry had one emblazoned on a flag: DONT GIVE UP THE SHIP. The other was Perry's report of the battle: "We have met the enemy and they are ours."

So Matthew Calbraith Perry had lived with a great tradition.

An earlier naval hero, James Lawrence, originally uttered the command "Don't give up the ship!" But by emblazoning it on this flag at the Battle of Lake Erie in 1813, Oliver Hazard Perry made the command famous.

But the mission to Japan called for qualities besides bravery and seamanship. It demanded initiative, scholarship and diplomacy. It was a delicate, ticklish assignment. Perry proved to be just the man for the job. He studied everything he could obtain on Japan, and he studied it so thoroughly that the government asked him to write his own instructions for the mission. He also took charge of selecting and assembling a remarkable array of gifts to take to the Emperor—gifts that were designed to show something about the United States and what it had to offer Japan. Into the holds of his ships went farm implements, telegraphs, a telescope; potatoes, whiskey and champagne; books and rifles and—most impressive of all—a working miniature train, complete with passenger car and tracks.

Perry had other qualifications for his mission, too. He was solidly built, with heavy, bushy eyebrows and firm features. Everyone regarded him as a strong, commanding figure. President Fillmore may well have thought that these qualities would make a powerful impression on the Japanese.

Flying the Stars and Stripes, the squadron sailed through the straits into Tokyo Bay on July 8, 1853. The commodore ignored or brushed aside attempts by Japanese sailors to board his ships or slow them down. He seems to have been keenly aware of the power these steamships represented as they towered over Japanese sailing vessels and, like dragons, belched smoke into the sky. After this visit, on which he presented his terms to the Japanese, Perry led his squadron to China. Then, in February 1854, he returned to Japan. His terms had been accepted. On March 31, 1854, the United States and the Japanese Empire signed a treaty of trade and friendship. This was the beginning of modern Japan.

During the next seven years, three more stars in the flag symbolized the admission of three more states. It was a thirty-four-star flag that came into being on July 4, 1861. But already, cannon had boomed at Fort Sumter in South Carolina, and the Civil War had begun. As the Southern states seceded from the Union, a new kind of flag question was asked. If a star was added to

At the beginning of the Civil War, the Stars and Stripes was hauled down at Fort Sumter, South Carolina. This picture shows the flag being raised after four years of war. The temporary staff was formed from an oar and a boat hook.

the flag each time a state was admitted, the question went, should a star be taken out of the flag when a state seceded? President Lincoln did not think so. His position was that the Union could not be broken—a state did not have the right to secede, whatever it claimed. Certainly the Government should not acknowledge acts of secession by removing stars from the American flag. Actually, the number of stars increased during the Civil War. West Virginia and Nevada became states, bringing the number to thirty-six.

The most notable flag developments of the Civil War were produced by the Confederacy. This was perfectly natural, of course, since the Confederacy was a brand-new government, with no flags or other official symbols. By March 1861, with remarkable speed, the Confederate States of America had acquired a national flag.

Even so, the Confederates seemed to have inherited the traditional vagueness of the United States Congress in flag matters. This new national flag was never technically adopted by the new government. It was nevertheless regarded by everyone as the official flag. It consisted of three broad horizontal stripes—red, white, red—and a blue canton with a star for each state. The Con-

The Stars and Bars—the unofficial Confederate national flag.

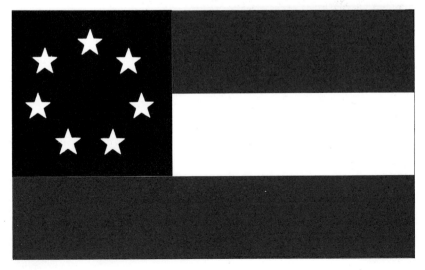

federates called these stripes "bars," and the flag became known as the Stars and Bars. At its peak the Confederacy claimed thirteen states, and this was the largest number of stars appearing in the canton of the Stars and Bars.

Although the name "Stars and Bars" is widely known today, a great many people do not think of the right flag when they hear it. Instead, they think of the best-known flag created in America except for the Stars and Stripes itself. This flag consists of a red field with a large blue saltire—the X-shaped cross—containing thirteen white stars along its arms. It is the flag nicknamed the "Southern Cross." It is this flag that most people now think of as the flag of the Confederacy. But it is not the Stars and Bars at all, and it never was the national flag of the Confederate States. It was the Confederate jack, and it flew from the bows of Confederate warships.

The basic design of this flag was created for use on battlefields. Southern generals felt that the Stars and Bars looked too much like the enemy Stars and Stripes to be a suitable battle flag. The new Battle Flag was a bold, eye-catching change. Nobody could mistake it for any other flag. When used as the Battle Flag, the Southern Cross was square, with a white border.

In 1863 the Confederate navy made the design official. They adopted it, in a rectangle instead of a square, as the jack. In square form the Southern Cross also became the canton of the ensign, which had a solid white field. At this same time, the Confederate Congress was getting around to deciding on an official national flag. As the war had gone on, many other persons besides the generals objected to the Stars and Bars. The design the Congress finally chose was the same as the ensign—the Battle Flag in the corner as the canton, and a solid white field.

A few weeks before Robert E. Lee's surrender to Ulysses S. Grant at Appomattox, the Confederates adopted one last flag. It really involved only a minor change in the 1863 national flag. The white field of the flag had caused problems because it sometimes looked like a plain white flag—a flag of surrender. So a

The "Southern Cross"—the most famous Confederate flag. Technically, this flag was the Confederate jack. If it was square with a white border, it was the Battle Flag.

The second Confederate flag (and first official national flag) : the Battle Flag in the canton, field of white.

A red stripe was added at the fly of the Confederacy's last flag so that it would not look like a flag of surrender.

vertical red stripe was added at the fly—the end away from the staff. But this flag saw little use. And, though it was the last national flag of the Confederacy, it was not the flag that everybody would remember a hundred years later. It was the brilliant, colorful Southern Cross that was still to be popular—and not only in the South—a century after the end of the Confederacy.

Three decades after the close of the Civil War, the U.S. Government decided that the cavalry as well as the artillery and the infantry should carry the Stars and Stripes as their standard. And in 1898, three years after this decision, the United States went to war with Spain. The war produced a famous cavalry leader who went on to become President. He was one of the most energetic men who have ever lived—a hunter, explorer, writer, politician, soldier. In this war with Spain he was a volunteer cavalry officer and he led a volunteer regiment, the Rough Riders. His exploits made his mustache, his eyeglasses, his toothy smile known across the country. Three years later, after the death of President McKinley, he became the twenty-sixth President of the United States.

During the war he was Colonel Theodore Roosevelt, United States Volunteers, serving in Cuba. His greatest fame came from the fiery way in which he led his regiment in an attack against the Spanish forces on the San Juan ridge, which defended the city of Santiago. The energetic colonel wanted to rush the Spanish, but he found his way blocked by another regiment. The soldiers of this regiment were sitting quietly, as if waiting for something.

"Why don't you charge?" Teddy Roosevelt asked their commanding officer.

"No orders yet."

"*I'll* give the orders," Roosevelt answered.

The other officer hesitated. Roosevelt suggested another solution: "You open up and let my men through."

This was done, and then many of the officers and men of the other regiment followed the Rough Riders and their colonel, who led the way.

Colonel (later President) Theodore Roosevelt was the fiery leader of the famed Rough Riders during the Spanish-American War. He liked to be in front of his men and usually was.

The flag that flew over the troops in Cuba contained in its blue canton a constellation of forty-five stars. Ten more states had joined the Union since the end of the Civil War. This flag flew until July 4, 1908, when a forty-sixth star was added, symbolizing the admission of Oklahoma.

The next year—1909—saw the completion of a flag adventure that had been undertaken fifteen years before. In the words of the man who lived it, it was the "last of the great adventure stories." This was, of course, a number of years before space exploration began. The story, he said, was told "under the folds of the Stars and Stripes, the flag that during a lonely and isolated life had come to be for me the symbol of home and everything I loved—and might never see again." The man was Robert Edwin Peary, the discoverer of the North Pole.

On all his Arctic expeditions for the previous fifteen years, he had carried a silk American flag wrapped around his body under his protective clothes. It had been made for him by his wife. On each expedition he had left a piece of this flag at the northernmost point he reached. Now, on April 6, 1909, he was standing at ninety degrees North latitude—the Pole itself. "The prize of three centuries," he wrote. "My dream and goal for twenty years. Mine at last!" And to symbolize the conquest of the Arctic, this dedicated explorer placed the rest of the cut-up flag in a sort of snow cave on a hummock of ice. He no longer needed to save it for future expeditions.

On July 4, 1912, two new stars appeared in the flag constellation. Arizona and New Mexico had come into the Union, completing the United States that stretched "from border to border and coast to coast"—from Canada to Mexico and from the Atlantic to the Pacific. This forty-eight-star flag has the distinction of being the longest-lived Stars and Stripes in American history. Our present-day fifty-star flag will have to fly until the year 2008 to outlast it. The forty-nine-star flag had exactly the opposite record. Its life-span was as short as an American flag's can be—one year, from July 4, 1959 (when Alaska's entry was symbolized), to July 4, 1960 (Hawaii).

Under the forty-eight-star flag, the United States moved fully into international affairs and became a great world power, far beyond anything the Founding Fathers could have dreamed of in 1776. Population and wealth increased enormously. New kinds of problems and challenges succeeded old ones. It was an era of great change and turmoil around the world. The United States fought in three major wars, the two World Wars and the Korean

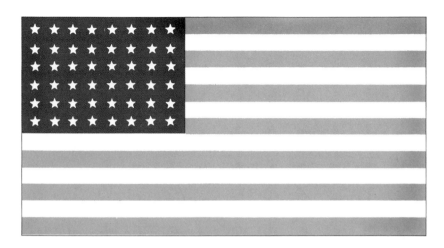

Adopted by order of President Taft on June 24, 1912, this forty-eight-star flag was the longest-lived version of the Stars and Stripes. It flew until 1959, when a forty-ninth star appeared for Alaska.

War. As we have seen, flags take on special significance in wartime. In the case of World War II, the flag was prominent at the very moment the United States entered the war.

It was one of the most famous days in our history: December 7, 1941. At Pearl Harbor, the great American naval base in Hawaii, the pride of the U.S. Navy lay at anchor—battleships, cruisers, destroyers and other ships. It was a clear, sunny morning, and everything was wrapped in Sunday quiet. But the signalmen in the Pearl Harbor tower were busy. At 0755 hours—five minutes till eight—they had broken out the "Prep" flag and bent it on its halyard. That was Navy talk for the act of taking the signal flag for the letter "P" from its locker and readying it to be raised. The raising of this "preparation" flag meant that in five minutes more, at 0800, the ceremony called Morning Colors would take place. This was the raising of the national ensign.

The Japanese attack on Pearl Harbor on December 7, 1941, created great destruction at the U.S. naval base. It was a sad and deadly day for the Stars and Stripes.

"Execute!" commanded the petty officer in charge of the signal detail.

Up went the "Prep" flag. In response to it, men lined up, ready for Morning Colors. But in those minutes a strange buzzing was heard in the sky. Planes with the Rising Sun of Japan painted on their wings roared overhead. Bullets slashed across parade areas, and torpedoes ripped into the moored battleships. It was a morning that would never be forgotten. The Stars and Stripes was under direct attack, and we were at war with Japan.

A little more than three years later, one of the fiercest battles of this Second World War was fought between American and Japanese forces. The Americans had been moving steadily across the Pacific, closer and closer to the Japanese homeland. "Island-hopping" was the name given to the U.S. strategy. Now, in February 1945, the U.S. Marines were going to assault the island of

Iwo Jima, 760 miles south of Tokyo. The purpose of attacking the island was to obtain bases from which the big B-29s could bomb Japan.

The presence of 21,000 Japanese defenders guaranteed that the battle would be ferocious. They had stiffened the island, which looked from above like a pork chop pointing south, with pillboxes and blockhouses from which to fire on the attackers. The island was full of caves in which the defenders could hide. But on February 19, after U.S. ships had bombarded Iwo Jima for three days, the first Marines landed.

The next day, in the narrow part of the pork chop, the 28th Marine Regiment launched an attack on the mountain that rose from the island. Mount Suribachi, it was called. Its code name was HOTROCKS.

By five o'clock in the afternoon the Marines had advanced two hundred bloody yards. Two more full days of savage fighting followed. But by ten o'clock on the morning of February 23, they stood in strength on the edge of the crater at the peak of HOT-ROCKS. Then they charged the remaining Japanese, and in a fierce skirmish they finished the battle for the mountain. Even before the skirmish was over, some members of the regiment's 2nd Battalion had picked up a piece of Japanese pipe, fastened a small American flag to it and had it ready to raise as soon as the shooting stopped.

But this flag was only twenty-eight inches by fifty-four inches. It was not big enough, some of the Marines felt, to fly over so hard-won a mountain. One of them went down a trail to the beach, obtained a flag from a ship and brought it back up the mountain. This was a good-sized flag—eight feet by four feet eight inches.

A photographer who happened to be nearby also came along. As the Marines raised this larger flag on Mount Suribachi, the photographer caught the scene. He produced a stirring picture, one of the great symbols of American victory. The picture has since served as the basis for stamps and statues. It was used as the

The Marines raise the flag on Mount Suribachi on the Pacific island of Iwo Jima. This great flag picture has itself become famous as an American symbol.

subject of the Marine Corps memorial, near the Arlington National Cemetery across the Potomac from Washington. This was fitting: as many as 6,800 Marines may have died on Iwo Jima, and about 18,000 were wounded. This statue, and the flag-raising itself, symbolize what was best and bravest in the American war efforts of this century.

7

The Nature of the Flag

FOR TWO CENTURIES now, the Stars and Stripes has flown over the United States. In good times and bad, in peace and war, it has been the symbol of the changing nation. It is as familiar to us as a close friend. We see it in front of school buildings, at baseball games, in churches and 240,000 miles away on the moon. Where facts about it have not been known, legends have been created—legends like the Betsy Ross story. But, as this book shows, the true story of the flag is a colorful and fascinating one.

Because the flag is the symbol of the nation, Americans have developed the custom of regarding it as a living thing and treating it with the courtesy and respect that should be shown to an honored person. This custom has not always been observed, of course. As was mentioned earlier, the flag has been attacked by people hostile to American deeds and policies. It has been treated casually by others, manufacturing companies and advertisers as well as individual persons. But everybody who uses the flag, whatever he uses it for, does so knowing that it is more than pieces of red, white and blue cloth sewn together. Its nature as a symbol is always with it. That is really the only true nature the flag has. It writes no laws and makes no policies. Like any other symbol, it has meaning in the minds of those who look at it, and nowhere else.

As you can see, a symbol is a thing of great power. Yet the United States Government has traditionally had a relaxed approach to questions concerning the flag. Over the years, rules for handling and displaying the flag have grown up, but they have not been developed by the Government, and throughout most of the flag's existence, they have not been official. There was not even a detailed description of the arrangement of the stars or of the proportions of the flag until 1912. In that year President William Howard Taft issued an executive order about the flag. It called for these proportions, which are still in effect:

Hoist (width) of flag	1
Fly (length) of flag	1.9
Hoist (width) of union	$\frac{7}{13}$
Fly (length) of union	0.76
Width of each stripe	$\frac{1}{13}$
Diameter of each star	.0616

This was very precise. But neither the President nor Congress adopted any rules concerning display of the flag. In the 1920s, following World War I, various patriotic organizations like the American Legion drew up codes of courtesy and use. But these were voluntary; they were not backed by law. It was not until 1942, in World War II, that Congress adopted an official Flag Code. The main points in this Code are given in Chapter 8.

In many countries of the world, it has long been a serious criminal offense to mutilate the flag, to tear it up or otherwise treat it with public disrespect. In the United States there was never any Federal law about this until 1968, when Congress declared such acts—they are called acts of desecration—a crime. But there has been a great deal of doubt and debate about this law.

The most honest tribute any flag—any symbol—can receive is tribute that is freely given. Our flag has waved over good deeds and bad ones. No one denies this. But as a symbol, this rectangle of bright-colored cloth stands (or ought to stand) for what is best in our history and traditions. It also reminds us that we have national ideals we must try to live by. It does not tell us we are perfect. It tells us we must always strive to be better. It is more than a symbol, really. It is a beacon.

8

The Flag Code

THESE RULES are based on the flag law adopted by Congress in 1942 and on the amendments later made to this law. The basic idea of the Flag Code is that the flag stands for a living country and is therefore regarded as though it were a living thing. The rules are based upon principles of courtesy and respect.

1. Normally, the flag should be displayed only from sunrise to sunset. But for special occasions it may be displayed at night. It should be raised briskly and lowered slowly and ceremoniously. Special days for flying the flag are New Year's Day, January 1; Presidential Inauguration Day, January 20; Lincoln's Birthday, February 12; Washington's Birthday;* Easter Sunday; Mother's Day, the second Sunday in May; Armed Forces Day, the third Saturday in May; Memorial Day* (half staff until noon); Flag Day, June 14; Independence Day, July 4; Labor Day, the first Monday in September; Citizenship Day, September 17; Columbus Day;* Veterans Day;* Thanksgiving Day, the fourth Thursday in November; Christmas Day, December 25.

* Each of these holidays has been made movable so that the observance is always on a Monday. Washington's Birthday is actually on February 22; Memorial Day used to be on May 30, Columbus Day on October 12, and Veterans Day on November 11.

The flag should not be flown in rainy or otherwise inclement weather.

2. When the flag is carried in a procession with another flag or flags, it should be either a) on the marching right—that is, the flag's own right—or b) in front of the center of the line of other flags.

3. When displayed with another flag against a wall from crossed staffs, the U.S. flag should be on the right. This means on the flag's own right, as it would look at you; your left, as you look at the flag. The staff of the U.S. flag should be in front of the staff of the other flag.

4. If the U.S. flag is in a group of flags (other than national flags) on separate staffs, it must be in the center and higher than the others.

5. If other flags are being flown on the same halyard, the U.S. flag must be at the peak. If it is in a line of flags, it must be on the right (again, its own right; your left, as you look at it).

6. If you are displaying flags of two or more nations, they should be flown from separate staffs of the same height and they should be of about the same size.

7. When the flag is displayed from a staff projecting from a building or a window, the union of the flag should go clear to the peak of the staff—unless the flag is supposed to be at half-staff.

8. When the flag is displayed flat against a wall—whether horizontally or vertically—the union should be uppermost and to the flag's own right. Here again, you see the importance of the idea of "the flag's own right." If the flag is in a window, it should be displayed in just the same way. The observer looking through the window from outside will see the blue union on *his* left.

9. When it is displayed over the middle of a street, the flag should be hung vertically. The union should be to the north in an east-west street, to the east in a north-south street.

10. When it is being displayed flat on a speaker's platform, the flag should be above and behind the speaker. If it is on a staff, it should be at the speaker's right—or, in church, on the minister's right. If it is out in the body of the auditorium or the church, however, it should be at the right of the audience or the congregation. There is a reason for this. When the flag is on the platform, the position of honor is at the speaker's right. When the flag is out on the floor of the auditorium, the position of honor is then the audience's right.

11. If you wish to drape a statue or a monument in preparation for an unveiling ceremony, do not use the flag as the covering. The law says, however, that the flag should "form a distinctive feature of the ceremony."

12. When the flag is to be flown at half-staff, you should first hoist it to the peak (the top) for an instant and then lower it to the half-staff position. Before lowering it at the end of the day, raise it again to the peak.

13. When the flag is used to cover a casket, it should be placed with the union at the head and over the left shoulder. It should not be lowered into the grave or allowed to touch the ground.

14. At no time should the flag touch anything beneath it—the ground, the floor, water or merchandise.

15. The flag should never be used as drapery or drawn back in any kind of folds. If the effect of drapery is wanted—on a speaker's platform, for instance—bunting of blue, white and red should be used (the blue always goes on top).

16. No writing, drawing or any other kind of marking should be placed on the flag.

17. The flag should not be used for any advertising purposes. It should not be embroidered on articles like cushions and handkerchiefs. It should not be printed on paper napkins, boxes or anything else designed to be used and thrown away. (See how long it takes you to find a violation of this rule.)

18. When the flag is no longer in fit condition to be displayed, it should not be casually thrown away or used for some other purpose. It should be "destroyed in a dignified way, preferably by burning."

9

Flag Talk

IMPORTANT WORDS AND THEIR MEANINGS

BANNER   Originally, *banners* were large, square standards or ensigns used by kings and important nobles. Now, as is the case with many flag words, the term has a number of meanings. One of the most common is simply *flag* (the Star-Spangled *Banner,* for instance).

BEDFORD FLAG   This very old Massachusetts flag is still in existence. Scholars believe that it was carried by the American Minutemen at the Battle of Concord on April 19, 1775.

BENNINGTON FLAG   This version of the U.S. flag had the number "76" in its canton. It is thought that this was the first Stars and Stripes to be used in battle (August 16, 1777).

CANTON   The rectangular area in the upper corner of a flag next to the staff is called the *canton*. In the U.S. flag, this is the blue field containing the white stars.

COLORS   Military flags are called colors and also standards. Originally, *colors* were carried by troops on foot and *standards* by mounted troops. The difference is not observed today.

CONTINENTAL COLORS   The unofficial flag of the United Colonies in 1775 and 1776 was called by several different names. One of the most common was *Continental Colors*. Most common of all, probably, was *Grand Union Flag*.

CONTINENTAL JACK   A number of Revolutionary flags used rattlesnakes to show American defiance of the British. The *Continental Jack* was one of these. It had thirteen red and white stripes, and the snake seemed to be crawling across them. There were also the words DONT TREAD ON ME.

ENSIGN   Nowadays, *ensign* generally means the most important flag a ship flies to show its nationality.

FIELD   This is the background part of a flag—the part on which designs and devices appear.

FLY   Like many other flag words, this has more than one meaning. The *fly* is the width of a flag, from left to right. The word is also used to describe the area of a flag farthest from the staff.

GOVERNMENT FLAG   In the United States, the *Government Flag* and the *National Flag* are the same—the Stars and Stripes. But some other countries have one flag that is supposed to be flown only by government officials and on government property and another flag that may be flown by private citizens. In Britain, for instance, the "Union Jack" is the government flag and private citizens are not supposed to fly it—but they often do. It is a historic and handsome flag. Who can blame them for liking it?

GRAND UNION FLAG   This is the same flag as the *Continental Colors*. It was flown by the rebelling colonies in 1775 and 1776 and by the new United States until the Stars and Stripes was adopted.

HALYARD   *Halyards* are the ropes that raise and lower flags.

HOIST   This, like *fly*, is one of the flag words with more than one meaning. The *hoist* is the height of a flag from top to bottom as you see it flying from a staff. The word also means the area of a flag closest to the staff—the part opposite the fly.

JACK   Along with the *ensign*, the *jack* shows the nationality of a ship. It is flown from a small staff at the bow.

MOULTRIE FLAG   A blue field with the word LIBERTY and a crescent moon in the canton. This was the flag flown by Colonel Moultrie at the Battle of Charleston in 1776. The battle saved this important port city from capture by the British.

NATIONAL FLAG   A flag that is supposed to be flown by the private citizens of a country is called the *National Flag*. In the United States it is the same as the *Government Flag*—the Stars and Stripes. In some countries the two kinds of flags are different.

OLD GLORY   This famous nickname is said to have been given to the U.S. flag by a Massachusetts sea captain named William Driver. In 1831, the story goes, Captain Driver was setting out on a voyage around the world. Some friends gave him an American flag as a farewell gift. As the flag was raised on his ship, the young captain (he was only twenty-one) said, "I'll call her Old Glory, boys, Old Glory!"

PHILADELPHIA LIGHT HORSE STANDARD   A cavalry troop called the Philadelphia Light Horse escorted General Washington part of the way from Philadelphia to Cambridge, Massachusetts, when he went to take command of the Continental Army. Their flag, or standard, is of special interest because it had in its canton thirteen blue and silver stripes. This use of stripes may have influenced the persons who created the Grand Union Flag.

POLE   In flag talk, a *pole* is not movable; it is planted permanently in the ground or fastened to a building. A *staff* is carried.

RED ENSIGN   This was the name of important British flags that flew in the colonies in the 1600s and 1700s. Today, the *Red Ensign* is the ensign flown by British merchant ships.

SALTIRE   St. Andrew's cross, shaped like a flattened-out X, is most properly called a *saltire*. In technical flag talk, a *cross* is upright.

STAFF   This is explained under POLE.

STANDARD   This term has even more meanings than most other flag words. In the ancient world a *standard* was not a flag but a rigid pole with a device of some kind on top. Later, a *royal standard* was a flag that accompanied a king on his travels. Cavalry units had *standards*. There are various other meanings, too.

STRIKE   The flag-talk meaning of *strike* is to lower a flag as a sign of surrender.

TEXEL FLAG   The flag with red, white and blue stripes flown by John Paul Jones is called the *Texel Flag* because he sailed to the Dutch island of Texel after the sinking of the *Bonhomme Richard*. Persons who saw the flag there wrote descriptions of it.

UNION   A *union* may be part of a flag or it may be an entire flag. Unions are designs or devices showing the coming-together of different crowns, states and the like. In the U.S. flag, the canton with its fifty stars is the union. In the British flag, the combination of crosses is itself a union device.

As the Flag Has Grown

DATES OF ADMISSION OF
THE FIFTY STATES

		Order of *Admission*
ALABAMA	December 14, 1819	22
ALASKA	January 3, 1959	49
ARIZONA	February 14, 1912	48
ARKANSAS	June 15, 1836	25
CALIFORNIA	September 9, 1850	31
COLORADO	August 1, 1876	38
CONNECTICUT	January 9, 1788	5
DELAWARE	December 7, 1787	1
FLORIDA	March 3, 1845	27
GEORGIA	January 2, 1788	4
HAWAII	August 21, 1959	50
IDAHO	July 3, 1890	43
ILLINOIS	December 3, 1818	21
INDIANA	December 11, 1816	19
IOWA	December 28, 1846	29
KANSAS	January 29, 1861	34

KENTUCKY	June 1, 1792	15
LOUISIANA	April 30, 1812	18
MAINE	March 15, 1820	23
MARYLAND	April 28, 1788	7
MASSACHUSETTS	February 6, 1788	6
MICHIGAN	January 26, 1837	26
MINNESOTA	May 11, 1858	32
MISSISSIPPI	December 10, 1817	20
MISSOURI	August 10, 1821	24
MONTANA	November 8, 1889	41
NEBRASKA	March 1, 1867	37
NEVADA	October 31, 1864	36
NEW HAMPSHIRE	June 21, 1788	9
NEW JERSEY	December 18, 1787	3
NEW MEXICO	January 6, 1912	47
NEW YORK	July 26, 1788	11
NORTH CAROLINA	November 21, 1789	12
NORTH DAKOTA	November 2, 1889	39
OHIO	March 1, 1803	17
OKLAHOMA	November 16, 1907	46
OREGON	February 14, 1859	33
PENNSYLVANIA	December 12, 1787	2
RHODE ISLAND	May 29, 1790	13
SOUTH CAROLINA	May 23, 1788	8
SOUTH DAKOTA	November 2, 1889	40
TENNESSEE	June 1, 1796	16
TEXAS	December 29, 1845	28
UTAH	January 4, 1896	45
VERMONT	March 4, 1791	14
VIRGINIA	June 25, 1788	10
WASHINGTON	November 11, 1889	42
WEST VIRGINIA	June 20, 1863	35
WISCONSIN	May 29, 1848	30
WYOMING	July 10, 1890	44

PICTURE CREDITS